Welcome

Bargello quilts look intricate, but you'll be surprised at how easy they are to make.

In this book, we present several methods for creating bargello quilts. All but two of the seven quilts can be completed by beginners or intermediate-level quilters. All of them have step-by-step instructions, so any quilter with an eye for detail and a bit of determination can make these beautiful designs.

Be sure to try the tube method, the mirrored-block method and the quilt-as-you-go method. Read the designer notes for tips and follow the many full-color figure drawings and instructions for making each quilt. You'll soon find that you love making bargello quilts. You'll also discover the secret that bargello quilts may look intricate and complex, but they are easy to make.

Table of Contents

3 Barjelly Table Cover

6 Mirage

12 Diamond Lites

21 Winter Whisper

26 Candy Hearts

31 Snowflake Jewels

36 Rugged High Country

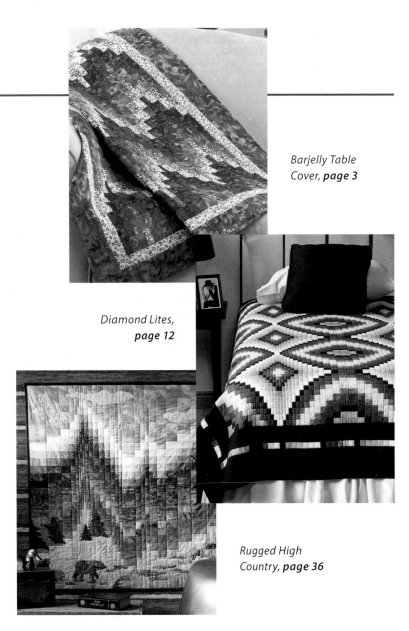

Barjelly Table Cover, page 3

Diamond Lites, page 12

Rugged High Country, page 36

House of White Birches, Berne, Indiana 46711   DRGnetwork.com

Barjelly Table Cover

By Julia Dunn

Using the tube method and Jelly Rolls™ for making bargello, this table cover or sofa throw is simple to stitch.

Project Specifications
Skill Level: Beginner
Project Size: 42¼" x 51"
Technique: Tube piecing

Materials
- ⅓ yard white print for first border
- 4—2½" x 42" strips each of 7 blue fabrics ranging from light (1) to dark (7) and numbered 1–7 or ⅜ yard each fabric
- 1 yard medium blue print for second border and binding
- Batting 49" x 57"
- Backing 49" x 57"
- Neutral color all-purpose thread
- Quilting thread
- Basic sewing tools and supplies

Cutting
1. If using yardage instead of precut strips, cut all seven fabrics into four 2½" by fabric width strips each.

2. Cut four 2" by fabric width D/E strips white print.

3. Cut five 3½" by fabric width F/G strips medium blue print.

4. Cut five 2¼" by fabric width binding strips medium blue print.

Completing the Strips
Note: *Press all seams open.*

1. Label all 2½"-wide strips numbers 1 through 7 with the No. 1 strip being the lightest and the No. 7 strip being the darkest.

2. Lay out the strips in same-number stacks from light to dark to make seven stacks.

3. Pick up one strip of each fabric and join in numerical order along length from light to dark to make a strip set as shown in Figure 1; press. Repeat to make four strip sets.

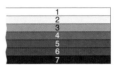
Figure 1

4. Join three of the strip sets along length, sewing the lightest strip of one strip set to the darkest strip of the second strip set to make three repeats in the color order; press.

5. Join the three strip-set unit to make a tube as shown in Figure 2; press.

Figure 2

6. Cut the remaining strip set across width into three equal pieces (each about 14" wide) as shown in Figure 3; join these pieces as in step 4 to make a narrower three-repeat strip set. Press.

Figure 3

7. Join to make a tube as in step 5; press.

8. Subcut the tubes into seven 1¼" A strips, (16) 1½" B strips and eight 2" C strips as shown in Figure 4.

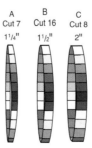

A	B	C
Cut 7	Cut 16	Cut 8
1¼"	1½"	2"

Figure 4

House of White Birches, Berne, Indiana 46711   DRGnetwork.com

Completing the Pieced Center

1. Lay out A, B and C tube strips in the following order: B, C, B, A, B, C, B. ***Note:*** *The strips are still sewn together in tubes.*

2. Leaving the strips arranged in the order given, pick up the first B strip. Remove the seam between pieces 4 and 5 to make a B1 strip as shown in Figure 5; lay the strip back down in its original placement.

3. Pick up the C strip; remove the seam between pieces 3 and 4, again referring to Figure 5 to make a C strip. Lay the strip back down in its original placement.

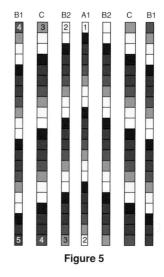

Figure 5

4. Pick up the next B strip; remove the seam between pieces 2 and 3 to make a B2 strip, again referring to Figure 5. Lay the strip back down in its original placement.

5. Pick up the A strip; remove the seam between pieces 1 and 2 to make an A1 strip, again referring to Figure 5. Lay the strip back down in its original placement.

6. Repeat steps 2–4 to make one more each B1, C and B2 strips, again referring to Figure 5.

7. Repeat steps 1–6 to lay out four sets of strips.

8. Remove the seam between pieces 5 and 6 on each of the three remaining A strips to make A2 strips as shown in Figure 6.

Completing the Pieced Top

1. Join the strips in the order shown in Figure 5 to make one design unit as shown in Figure 7; press. Repeat to make four design units.

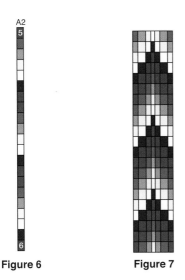

Figure 6	Figure 7

2. Join the design units with the A2 strips as shown in Figure 8 to complete the pieced center; press.

Figure 8

3. Join the D/E strips on short ends to make one long strip; press seams open. Subcut strip into two 42½" D strips and two 36¾" E strips.

4. Sew a D strip to opposite long sides and E strips to the top and bottom of the pieced center; press seams toward D and E strips.

5. Join the F/G strips on short ends to make one long strip; press seams open. Subcut strip into two 45½" F strips and two 42¾" G strips.

6. Sew an F strip to opposite long sides and G strips to the top and bottom of the pieced center to complete the pieced top; press seams toward F and G strips.

Finishing the Quilt

1. Sandwich batting between the completed top and prepared backing piece; pin or baste layers together to hold flat.

2. Quilt as desired by hand or machine; remove pins or basting. Trim batting and backing even with the top.

3. Join the binding strips with right sides together on short ends to make one long strip; press seams open.

4. Press the strip in half with wrong sides together along length.

5. Sew the binding to the quilt edges, mitering corners and overlapping ends.

6. Fold binding to the back side and stitch in place to finish. ❖

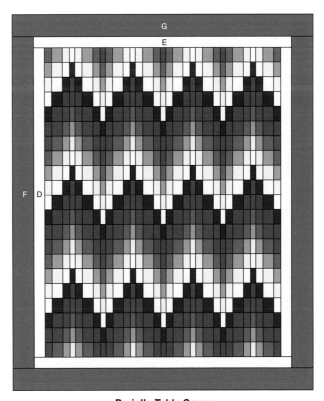

Barjelly Table Cover
Placement Diagram 42¼" x 51"

Mirage

By Dereck C. Lockwood

Bargello takes on a whole new dimension in this beautiful quilt.

Designer Notes

My method of making the center panel of this quilt is quite easy. You will be making multicolored panels from strips of fabrics. Then you will cut strips from these panels across all the colors to a specified size for each required row.

The strips are sewn end-to-end, eliminating certain colors and/or adding other colors as you follow the colored chart, working one row at a time. As you complete each row, it will be sewn to the preceding row until you have finished the center panel. After all this is done, then you only have to add your border to the top, and it is ready to quilt.

If this is your first time using my bargello technique, it will go rather slowly at first until you get used to it.

When sewing strips together to make panels, use a smaller stitch length than usual so the stitches don't pull apart when you are handling and sewing the cut strips together later. Use a scant ¼" seam

FABRIC Measurements based on 42" usable fabric width. All fabrics are tonals.	#STRIPS & PIECES	CUT
⅛ yard light lavender	2	1½" x 42"
⅛ yard medium lavender	2	1½" x 42"
⅛ yard deep lavender	2	1½" x 42"
⅛ yard light violet	2	1½" x 42"
⅛ yard medium violet	2	1½" x 42"
⅛ yard deep violet	2	1½" x 42"
¼ yard light rose	3	1½" x 42"
¼ yard medium rose	3	1½" x 42"
¼ yard light blue	4	1½" x 42"
¼ yard medium blue	4	1½" x 42"
¼ yard deep blue	4	1½" x 42"
¼ yard light gold	3	1½" x 42"
¼ yard medium gold	3	1½" x 42"
¼ yard deep gold	3	1½" x 42"

FABRIC Measurements based on 42" usable fabric width. All fabrics are tonals.	#STRIPS & PIECES	CUT
¼ yard light green	3	1½" x 42"
¼ yard medium green	3	1½" x 42"
¼ yard medium deep green	3	1½" x 42"
¼ yard dark green	3	1½" x 42"
¼ yard light olive green	3	1½" x 42"
¼ yard medium olive green	3	1½" x 42"
¼ yard deep olive green	3	1½" x 42"
⅜ yard deep rose	6	1½" x 42"
1⅜ yards off-white solid	7 2 3 5	1½" x 42" 4½" x 39½" A 4½" x 42" B 2¼" x 42" binding
Backing		53" x 53"

SUPPLIES

- Batting 53" x 53"
- Neutral color all-purpose thread
- Quilting thread
- Basic sewing tools and supplies

allowance when sewing so the quilt will be close to the correct size when the quilt top is finished. It is very important that you use an exact and consistent seam throughout so that all seams match. The strips are narrow in size when stitched, and it is easy to have mismatched seams.

When cutting strips from yardage, use a 24" or larger-size cutting mat and a 24"-long ruler. When recutting into narrow strips, I prefer to use a 12"-long ruler.

Square up the cut edge of your fabric with the fold of the fabric (not the selvage) so you don't get a wave in your cut strip. I do not recommend folding the fabric twice because you are increasing your chances of getting wavy strips when they are opened.

Use a steam iron for all pressing.

Project Specifications
Skill Level: Advanced
Project Size: 47" x 47"
Technique: Strip piecing

Completing the Strip-Pieced Panels
Note: Press seams in all pieced panels in one direction. It doesn't matter which direction, because they will be pressed again later.

1. Join one strip each dark green, medium deep green, medium green, light green, light olive green, medium olive green and deep olive green with right sides together along length in the order given and as shown in Figure 1; repeat to make three green panels.

Make 3

Figure 1

2. Join strips for rose panels in the following order referring to Figure 2: light rose, medium rose, deep rose, off-white and deep rose. Repeat to make three rose panels.

Make 3

Figure 2

3. Join strips for lavender panels in the following order referring to Figure 3: light lavender, medium lavender and deep lavender. Repeat to make two lavender panels.

Make 2

Figure 3

4. Join strips for violet panels in the following order referring to Figure 4: light violet, medium violet and deep violet. Repeat to make two violet panels.

Make 2

Figure 4

5. Join strips for blue panels in the following order referring to Figure 5: light blue, medium blue, deep blue and off-white. Repeat to make four blue panels.

Make 4

Figure 5

6. Join strips for gold panels in the following order referring to Figure 6: light gold, medium gold and deep gold. Repeat to make three gold panels.

Make 3

Figure 6

Creating Rows for Pieced Top
Note: When all rows are completed and joined, the Row 1 edge of the pieced center will be the left edge of the quilt as shown in the Placement Diagram.

1. Select a panel of each color. Clip a legal-size envelope or piece of paper to the page for Figure 7 so the top edge of the envelope or paper is directly below Row 1 and most of the rest of the chart is covered. This makes it easier to see what is needed for that row and to sew the correct strips or segments together for just that row. Move the envelope or paper down to other rows as you progress through the steps.

2. Looking at Row 1, note that you need two green strips for this row—for the green sections at each end of the row; cut two 1⅜" strips from a green panel.

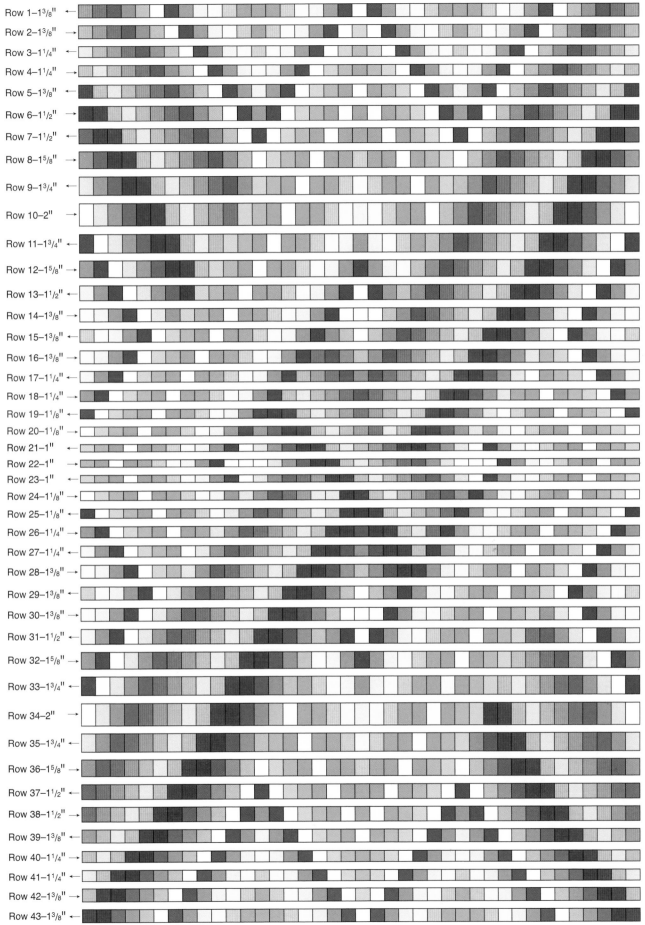

Row 1–1³⁄₈" ←
Row 2–1³⁄₈" →
Row 3–1¹⁄₄" ←
Row 4–1¹⁄₄" →
Row 5–1³⁄₈" ←
Row 6–1¹⁄₂" →
Row 7–1¹⁄₂" ←
Row 8–1⁵⁄₈" →
Row 9–1³⁄₄" ←
Row 10–2" →
Row 11–1³⁄₄" ←
Row 12–1⁵⁄₈" →
Row 13–1¹⁄₂" ←
Row 14–1³⁄₈" →
Row 15–1³⁄₈" ←
Row 16–1³⁄₈" →
Row 17–1¹⁄₄" ←
Row 18–1¹⁄₄" →
Row 19–1¹⁄₈" ←
Row 20–1¹⁄₈" →
Row 21–1" ←
Row 22–1" →
Row 23–1" ←
Row 24–1¹⁄₈" →
Row 25–1¹⁄₈" ←
Row 26–1¹⁄₄" →
Row 27–1¹⁄₄" ←
Row 28–1³⁄₈" →
Row 29–1³⁄₈" ←
Row 30–1³⁄₈" →
Row 31–1¹⁄₂" ←
Row 32–1⁵⁄₈" →
Row 33–1³⁄₄" ←
Row 34–2" →
Row 35–1³⁄₄" ←
Row 36–1⁵⁄₈" →
Row 37–1¹⁄₂" ←
Row 38–1¹⁄₂" →
Row 39–1³⁄₈" ←
Row 40–1¹⁄₄" →
Row 41–1¹⁄₄" ←
Row 42–1³⁄₈" →
Row 43–1³⁄₈" ←

Figure 7

House of White Birches, Berne, Indiana 46711   DRGnetwork.com

3. Again looking at Row 1, note that you need two violet, four blue, four gold and one rose strips to complete the row; cut the required number of 1⅜"-wide strips from the appropriate color panels for these strips.

4. Gather the cut strips, the color chart and your seam ripper and move to your sewing machine.

5. Following Row 1 on the chart, pick up a green strip; note that all you need from this strip are the dark green and medium deep green pieces. Rip out the seam between the medium green and the medium deep green pieces as shown in Figure 8; set the leftover green strip aside. *Note: Save the leftover sections; you may be able to use them later.*

Figure 8

6. Place the dark green piece on your sewing machine and look at the color chart again to see that you will next need a complete violet strip. Sew the deep violet end of the strip to the medium deep green end of the green unit as shown in Figure 9 to make the beginning of the row.

Figure 9

7. Sew the off-white end of a blue strip to the light violet end of the stitched unit; sew the light gold piece to the light blue piece. Remove a deep rose piece from the rose strip; set aside remainder of the rose strip and sew the deep rose piece to the deep gold piece. Add a blue strip as shown in Row 1; you are now at the center of the row. Continue, using another blue strip, remove the off-white piece and sew the deep blue end to the row. Continue along the row referring to Figure 7. For the second deep rose piece, remove it from the rose strip used before; set the remainder of the rose strip aside. Continue to complete Row 1. Double-check colors against Row 1 in Figure 7 and make any corrections needed.

8. Re-press all seams toward the left end of the row; label as Row 1 and set aside. *Note: All odd-numbered rows will have seams re-pressed toward the left end and all even-numbered rows will have seams re-pressed toward the right end as indicated by the arrows in Figure 7. This makes the seams interlock when the rows are stitched together later.*

9. Slide the envelope or paper down on the Figure 7 chart so that Row 2 is uncovered; note that you will need two green strips, two violet strips, four blue strips and four gold strips cut 1⅜"-wide from the panels. You will also note that you need only one light rose piece; this may be removed from the leftover strip from step 7 above.

10. Take these strips to your sewing machine along with Figure 7 chart, and sew the row together as in previous steps, adding and/or removing pieces as necessary to make Row 2. Re-press seams in this row toward the right end.

11. Take Rows 1 and 2 to the sewing machine; place Row 1 faceup on the bed of the machine and Row 2 facedown on top of it. Stitch these two rows together, making sure the seams interlock with each other tightly. Press seam toward Row 1.

12. Prepare chart to stitch Row 3. Check the chart to see that you will need two green, two violet, four blue, two gold and two rose strips cut 1¼" wide from panels.

13. Sew these together, adding or removing pieces as necessary to complete the row according to the chart; press seams toward the left end. Sew Row 3 to the stitched unit. *Note: Hold Row 3 alongside Row 2; if both rows are the same length, you are ready to sew them together. If Row 3 is longer or shorter, then you have made an error.*

14. Row 4 strips are cut 1¼" wide. You will need two green, two violet, four blue and two rose strips.

15. Sew Row 4 together following the chart; press seams toward the right end. Sew the row to Row 3; press seam toward Row 3. *Note: Up until this point, the rows have been mirror images from the center to each side so it didn't matter if you made an error in re-pressing the seams. That will start to change when you reach Row 9. The rows will then have different ends, so pay close attention to the pressing arrows in the chart.*

16. Continue moving envelope or paper down the rows and cutting panel strips as directed on the cutting chart for width and color, being very careful to cut strips the right size. Then complete and join rows as you stitch to complete the pieced center.

Completing the Pieced Top

1. Sew an A strip to opposite sides of the pieced center; press seams toward A strips.

2. Join the B strips on short ends to make one long strip; press seams open. Subcut strip into two 47½" B strips.

3. Sew a B strip to the remaining sides of the pieced center; press seams toward B strips to complete the pieced top.

Finishing the Quilt

1. Sandwich batting between the completed top and prepared backing piece; pin or baste layers together to hold flat.

2. Quilt as desired by hand or machine; remove pins or basting. Trim batting and backing even with the top. *Note: The quilt shown was machine-quilted in the ditch of the seams of the quilt center, first quilting from top to bottom and then from side to side. The border designs were stitched and then stipple-quilted in the space surrounding the stitched design and in all off-white squares in the quilt center.*

3. Join the binding strips with right sides together on short ends to make one long strip; press seams open.

4. Press the strip in half with wrong sides together along length.

5. Sew the binding to the quilt edges, mitering corners and overlapping ends.

6. Fold binding to the back side and stitch in place to finish. ❖

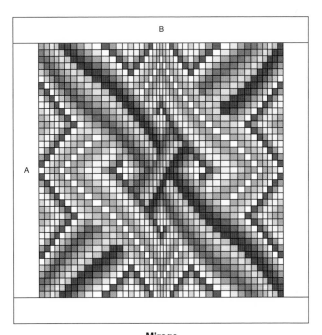

Mirage
Placement Diagram 47" x 47"

Diamond Lites

By Dereck C. Lockwood

A repeating block design lets you make this strip-pieced bargello-design quilt in a range of sizes.

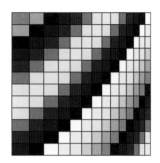

A
12" x 12" Block
Make 12 (48, 64)

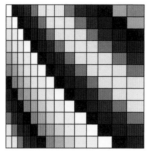

B
12" x 12" Block
Make 12 (48, 64)

Designer Notes

Unlike my other bargello designs, which are made basically in long strips from top to bottom, this quilt is made from two basic mirror-image 12"-square blocks. This method enables you to make the design in various sizes. I have included instructions for making this quilt in a 66" x 90" topper, and in parentheses, a 90" x 114" queen-size quilt and 114"-square king-size quilt.

The quilt is made from six shades of amber and five shades of green, each ranging from light to dark. You may substitute any colors for these two that suit the person or room that you are making it for. You may use solid, mottled or tonal fabrics that will give you the range of shades that you need. For example, if you change the greens to silver-grays and the yellows to shades of rose, you could change the black background to a very dark burgundy.

When making this decision, lay out all the shades of the two selected colors and try different colors for the background between them until you find one that makes your fabrics "pop." Even a cream fabric will work with a lot of colors to give you a lighter look. Just remember that your background fabric must work as an accent and as an outline to the diamond and pillow shapes within the quilt so that they don't melt into one another.

Be sure to label your fabrics as indicated in the Materials list and again as 1½"-wide strips are cut

for strip piecing. These numbers are referred to throughout the instructions and drawings.

Figures 1, 2 and 3 show stitching for panels 1, 2 and 3, and subcutting these panels into 2"-wide Strips 1 and 28, 1¾"-wide Strips 2 and 27 and 1¾"-wide Strips 3 and 26.

Figure 4 shows the sequences in which fabrics (by fabric number) are stitched for panels 4–14 and the widths that Strips 4/25–14/15 are subcut from the panels. Only the black pieces are filled in this figure, because it makes it easier to see the pattern at a glance and gives a visual reference point. Each strip is made up of 12 pieces. Also the strips are cut in a variety of widths to create the curved design within each block. Refer to this figure when piecing all blocks.

Project Specifications

Skill Level: Advanced
Project Size: 66" x 90" (90" x 114" and 114" x 114")
Block Size: 12" x 12"
Number of Blocks: 24 (48, 64)
Technique: Strip piecing

Materials (queen, king)

- ½ (1, 1⅛) yard pale green (No. 1)
- ⅝ (1, 1⅛) yard medium amber (No. 8)
- ½ (⅞, 1) yard medium deep amber (No. 9)
- ½ (⅞, ⅞) yard very deep amber (No. 11)
- ⅝ (1⅛, 1⅜) yard pale amber (No. 6)
- ⅝ (1⅛, 1¼) yard light amber (No. 7)
- ⅝ (1, 1⅛) yard deep amber (No. 10)
- 1 (1¾, 2¼) yard light green (No. 2)
- 1 (1⅞, 2⅓) yard medium green (No. 3)
- 1⅛ (1⅞, 2⅜) yards deep green (No. 4)
- 1⅛ (2, 2½) yards dark green (No. 5)
- 3½ (5¼, 6) yards black solid (No. 12 background)
- Batting 72" x 96" (96" x 120", 120" x 120")
- Backing 72" x 96" (96" x 120", 120" x 120")
- Neutral color and black all-purpose thread
- Quilting thread
- Basic sewing tools and supplies

Completing Panel 1, Strips 1 & 28

Note: When making block A, you will also be precutting the strips for block B and setting them aside for later use. Full instructions are included for Strips 1 and 28; limited instructions will follow for remaining strips, as they are all made using the same method with color-placement changes and recutting sizes.

1. Cut 1½" by fabric width strips from fabrics 1, 2, 3, 4, 5, 10, 11 and 12 as listed:

Fabric	Topper	Queen	King
1	2	3	4
2	4	6	8
3	4	6	8
4	4	6	8
5	4	6	8
10	2	3	4
11	2	3	4
12	2	3	4

2. Sew strip 11 right sides together along the length with strip 10; press seam toward strip 10. Sew strip 12 to the strip 10 side of the stitched strip; press seam toward strip 12.

3. Continue sewing strips to the stitched panel in this manner in the following order to make panel 1 referring to Figure 1: 5, 4, 3, 2, 1, 2, 3, 4, 5; press all seams toward the most recently added strip after each addition.

Panel 1
Strips 1/28
2"

Figure 1

4. Repeat to make two (3, 4) of these panels.

5. Square-up ends of panels and subcut into 24 (48, 64) 2" segments, again referring to Figure 1. *Note: You may need to trim the ends several times as you are cutting the segments to keep straight seams along each segment. You will have sections of the panels left over; place these aside, as you will use some of them in border 2.*

6. Stack 12 (24, 32) segments, keeping piece 11 at the top, and label it Strip 1; re-press seams of the remaining 12 (24, 32) segments toward the top of the strip. Label these as Strip 28; set aside for B blocks.

Completing Panel 2, Strips 2 & 27

1. Cut 1½" by fabric width strips from fabrics as listed:

Fabric	Topper	Queen	King
12	2	4	6
5	2	4	6
4	2	4	6
3	2	4	6
2	2	4	6
1	1	2	3
10	1	2	3

2. Referring to Figure 2 and stitching from top to bottom, sew strips right sides together along length to make panel 2; press seams toward the top of the panel. *Note: When making the panels, the seams are pressed down on all odd-numbered panels. The seams are pressed up on all even-numbered panels.*

Panel 2
Strips 2/27
1¾"

Figure 2

3. Square-up the ends of the stitched panel and subcut into 24 (48, 64) 1¾" segments.

4. Select 12 (24, 32) segments, label Strip 2, pin together and set aside. Re-press seams of remaining 12 (24, 32) strips toward the bottom; label these Strip 27 and set aside for B blocks.

5. To begin piecing A blocks, place a Strip 1 faceup on the sewing machine, making sure fabric piece 11 is at the top; place Strip 2, with piece 10 at the top, right sides together on Strip 1 and sew together, interlocking seams. Press seam toward Strip 2. Repeat with remaining Strips 1 and 2 to begin piecing 12 (24, 32) A blocks. *Note: All seams in block A will be pressed from the lowest to the highest numbered strips.*

Completing Panel 3, Strips 3 & 26

1. Cut 1½" by fabric width strips from fabrics as listed:

Fabric	Topper	Queen	King
12	2	4	6
5	2	4	6
4	2	4	6
3	2	4	6
2	2	4	6
1	1	2	3
6	1	2	3

2. Referring to Figure 3, complete panel 3 as for panels 1 and 2, press seams toward panel bottom. Complete one panel for topper, two for queen and three for king.

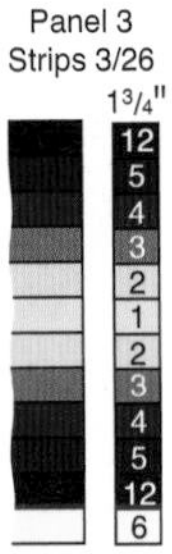
Panel 3
Strips 3/26
1¾"
12
5
4
3
2
1
2
3
4
5
12
6

Figure 3

3. Square-up the end of panel(s) and subcut into (24) 1¾" segments for topper, 48 for queen and 64 for king.

4. Label half of the segments Strip 3. Re-press seams up on the remaining strips and label Strip 26; set aside for block B.

5. Sew Strip 3 to the Strip 2 side of the previously stitched A block sections; press seam toward Strip 3.

Completing Panel 4, Strips 4 & 25

1. Cut 1½" by fabric width strips from fabrics as listed:

Fabric	Topper	Queen	King
12	1	2	3
5	2	4	6
4	2	4	6
3	2	4	6
2	2	4	6
1	1	2	3
6	1	2	3
7	1	2	3

2. Referring to Figure 4, stitch to make one (2, 3) panel(s) 4.

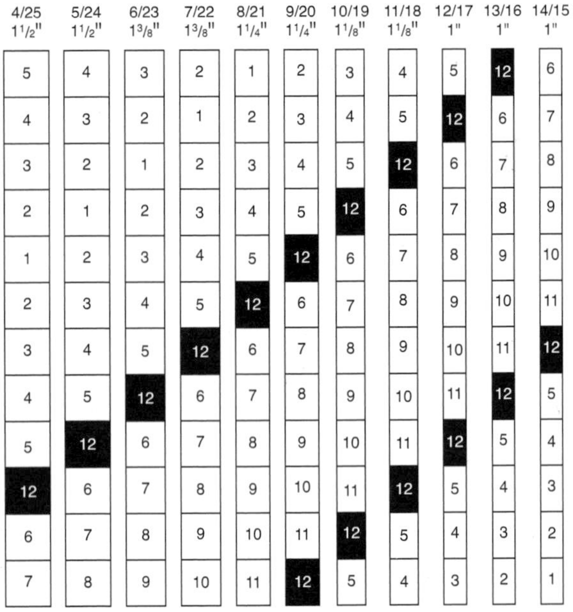
4/25 1½": 5 4 3 2 1 2 3 4 5 12 6 7
5/24 1½": 4 3 2 1 2 3 4 5 12 6 7 8
6/23 1⅜": 3 2 1 2 3 4 5 12 6 7 8 9
7/22 1⅜": 2 1 2 3 4 5 12 6 7 8 9 10
8/21 1¼": 1 2 3 4 5 12 6 7 8 9 10 11
9/20 1¼": 2 3 4 5 12 6 7 8 9 10 11 12
10/19 1⅛": 3 4 5 12 6 7 8 9 10 11 12 5
11/18 1⅛": 4 5 12 6 7 8 9 10 11 12 5 4
12/17 1": 5 12 6 7 8 9 10 11 12 5 4 3
13/16 1": 12 6 7 8 9 10 11 12 5 4 3 2
14/15 1": 6 7 8 9 10 11 12 5 4 3 2 1

Figure 4

3. Square-up the end of the stitched panel and subcut into 24 (48, 64) 1½" segments.

4. Label half the segments Strip 4; re-press seams of remaining segments down and label Strip 25; set aside for B blocks.

5. Sew Strip 4 to Strip 3 side of A block sections; press seams toward Strip 4.

Completing Panel 5, Strips 5 & 24

1. Cut 1½" by fabric width strips from fabrics as listed:

Fabric	Topper	Queen	King
4	2	4	6
3	2	4	6
2	2	4	6
1	1	2	3
5	1	2	3
12	1	2	3
6	1	2	3
7	1	2	3
8	1	2	3

2. Again referring to Figure 4, make one (2, 3) panel(s) 5; press seams down.

3. Subcut 24 (48, 64) 1½" segments from panel; select 12 (24, 32) segments for Strip 5; re-press seams up on remaining segments, label as Strip 24 and set aside for block B.

4. Sew Strip 5 to Strip 4 on stitched A block sections; press seams toward Strip 5.

Completing Panel 6, Strips 6 & 23

1. Cut 1½" by fabric width strips from fabrics as listed:

Fabric	Topper	Queen	King
3	2	4	6
2	2	4	6
1	1	2	3
4	1	2	3
5	1	2	3
12	1	2	3
6	1	2	3
7	1	2	3
8	1	2	3
9	1	2	3

2. Again referring to Figure 4, make one (2, 3) panel(s) 6; press seams up.

3. Subcut panel into 24 (48, 64) 1⅜" segments; label half Strip 6. Label remainder Strip 23, re-press seams down and set aside for B blocks.

4. Sew Strip 6 to Strip 5 on A block sections; press seams toward Strip 6.

Completing Panel 7, Strips 7 & 22

1. Cut two (4, 6) 1½" by fabric width strips from fabric 2 and one (2, 3) from each of the following fabrics: 1, 3, 4, 5, 12, 6, 7, 8, 9 and 10.

2. Again referring to Figure 4, make one (2, 3) panel(s) 7; press seams down.

3. Subcut panel into 24 (48, 64) 1⅜" segments; label half Strip 7. Label remainder Strip 22; re-press seams and set aside. Sew Strip 7 to Strip 6 on A block sections; press seams toward Strip 7.

Completing Panel 8, Strips 8 & 21

1. Cut one (2, 2) 1½" by fabric width strips from fabrics 1 through 12.

2. Again referring to Figure 4, make one (2, 2) panel(s) 8; press seams up.

3. Subcut panel into 24 (48, 64) 1¼" segments; label half Strip 8. Label remainder Strip 21; re-press seams and set aside. Sew Strip 8 to Strip 7 on A block sections; press seams toward Strip 8.

Completing Panel 9, Strips 9 & 20

1. Cut one (2, 2) 1½" by fabric width strips from fabrics 2 through 11 and two (4, 4) from fabric 12.

2. Again referring to Figure 4, make one (2, 2) panel(s) 9; press seams down.

3. Subcut panel into 24 (48, 64) 1¼" segments; label half Strip 9. Label remainder Strip 20; re-press seams and set aside. Sew Strip 9 to Strip 8 on A block sections; press seams toward Strip 9.

Completing Panel 10, Strips 10 & 19

1. Cut one (2, 2) 1½" by fabric width strips from fabrics 3 and 4, and 6 through 11 and two (4, 4) from fabrics 12 and 5.

2. Again referring to Figure 4, make one (2, 2) panel(s) 10; press seams up.

3. Subcut panel into 24 (48, 64) 1⅛" segments; label half Strip 10. Label remainder Strip 19; re-press seams and set aside. Sew Strip 10 to Strip 9 on A block sections; press seams toward Strip 9.

Completing Panel 11, Strips 11 & 18

1. Cut one (2, 2) 1½" by fabric width strips from fabrics 6 through 11 and two (4, 4) from fabrics 12, 5 and 4.

2. Again referring to Figure 4, make one (2, 2) panel(s) 11; press seams down.

3. Subcut panel into 24 (48, 64) 1⅛" segments; label half Strip 11. Label remainder Strip 18; re-press seams and set aside. Sew Strip 11 to Strip 10 on A block sections; press seams toward Strip 11.

Completing Panel 12, Strips 12 & 17

1. Cut one (2, 2) 1½" by fabric width strips from fabrics 3 and 4, and 6 through 11 and two (4, 4) from fabrics 12 and 5.

2. Again referring to Figure 4, make one (2, 2) panel(s) 12; press seams up.

3. Subcut panel into 24 (48, 64) 1" segments; label half Strip 12. Label remainder Strip 17; re-press seams and set aside. Sew Strip 12 to Strip 11 on A block sections; press seams toward Strip 12.

18

Completing Panel 13, Strips 13 & 16

1. Cut one (2, 2) 1½" by fabric width strips from fabrics 2 through 11 and two (4, 4) from fabric 12.

2. Again referring to Figure 4, make one (2, 2) panel(s) 13; press seams down.

3. Subcut panel into 24 (48, 64) 1" segments; label half Strip 13. Label remainder Strip 16; re-press seams and set aside. Sew Strip 13 to Strip 12 on A block sections; press seams toward Strip 13.

Completing Panel 14, Strips 14 & 15

1. Cut one (2, 2) 1½" by fabric width strips from fabrics 1 through 12.

2. Again referring to Figure 4, make one (2, 2) panel(s) 14; press seams up.

3. Subcut panel into 24 (48, 64) 1" segments; label half Strip 14. Label remainder Strip 15; re-press seams and set aside. Sew Strip 14 to Strip 13 on A block sections to complete the A blocks; press seams toward Strip 14.

Completing B Blocks

1. Sew Strip 16 to Strip 15; press seam toward Strip 16. Continue sewing strips in reverse numerical order referring to Figure 5, pressing seam toward the newly added strip after each addition to make 12 (24, 32) B blocks.

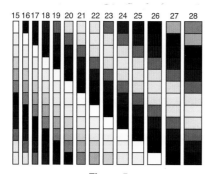

Figure 5

Completing the Pieced Center

1. Sew one A block to one B block as shown in Figure 6; repeat, reversing position of block, again referring to Figure 6. Press seams in the block rows in opposite directions.

2. Join the block rows to complete a block unit as shown in Figure 7; press seam in one direction. Repeat to make six (12, 16) block units.

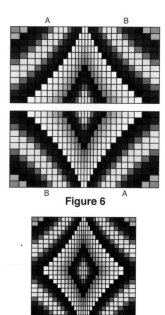

Figure 6

Figure 7

3. Join two (3, 4) block units to make a row; press seam in one direction. Repeat to make three (4, 4) rows.

Diamond Lites Topper
Placement Diagram 66" x 90"

4. Join the rows with seams in opposite directions to complete the pieced center. *Note: Refer to the Placement Diagrams for queen and king sizes for arrangement of blocks, joining in the same manner.*

Adding Borders

1. Cut seven (9, 10) 3½" by fabric width strips black solid. Join strips on short ends to make one long strip; press seams open.

2. Subcut strip into two each 72½" (96½", 96½") C strips and 54½" (78½", 102½") D strips.

3. Cut seven (10, 11) 5½" by fabric width strips black solid. Join strips on short ends to make one long strip; press seams open.

4. Subcut strip into two each 80½" (104½", 104½") E strips and 66½" (90½", 114½") F strips.

5. Sew a C strip to opposite long sides and D strips to the top and bottom of the pieced center; press seams toward C and D strips.

6. Subcut remaining panels into 1½" segments, trying to use segments with all six colors of amber and all six colors of green with the black.

7. Join the segments starting with black, then amber (light to dark), black, then green (light to dark), repeating the sequence to create one strip at least 280" (380", 430") long; press seams toward black.

8. Begin sewing the strip to one long side, trimming excess at end; press seam toward C strip. Repeat on the opposite side and then on the top and bottom.

9. Sew an E strip to opposite long sides and F strips to the top and bottom of the pieced center to complete the pieced top; press seams toward E and F strips.

Finishing the Quilt

1. Sandwich batting between the completed top and prepared backing piece; pin or baste layers together to hold flat.

2. Quilt as desired by hand or machine; remove pins or basting. Trim batting and backing even with the pieced top.

3. Cut eight (10, 12) 2¼" by fabric width strips black solid for binding. Join strips with right sides together on short ends to make one long strip; press seams open.

4. Press the strip in half with wrong sides together along length.

5. Sew the binding to the quilt edges, mitering corners and overlapping ends.

6. Fold binding to the back side and stitch in place to finish. ❖

Diamond Lites Queen
Placement Diagram 90" x 114"

Diamond Lites King
Placement Diagram 114" x 114"

House of White Birches, Berne, Indiana 46711   DRGnetwork.com

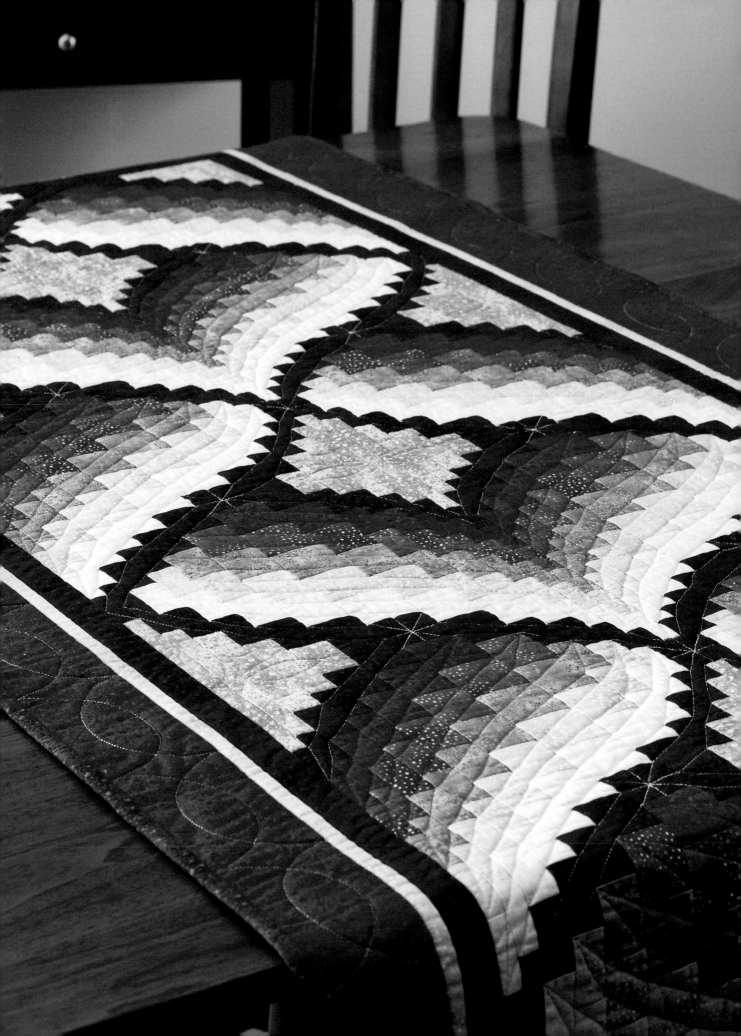

Winter Whisper

Design by Colleen Reale & Chloe Anderson of Toadusew

Quilted by Asta Dorset

Cool blue colors combine with dark blue and teal to create a ribbon-like design.

Designer Notes

Labeling and organizing pieces and units as they are listed will prevent confusion later.

An accurate ¼" seam allowance is critical when strip piecing and should be verified prior to sewing.

FABRIC Measurements based on 42" (WOF) usable fabric width. S = spacer SPU = strip-pieced unit	#STRIPS & PIECES	CUT	#PIECES	SUBCUT
⅓ yard color 3 medium-dark blue tonal*	1 3	2" x WOF 2" x WOF (SPU 1)	1	21" (SPU 5)
⅓ yard color 4 medium blue tonal*	1 3	2" x WOF 2" x WOF (SPU 1)	1 1 1	21" (SPU 5) 18" (SPU 4) 1" x 1¼" (S15)
⅜ yard navy tonal*	4	2¼" x WOF binding		
⅜ yard color 5 light blue tonal*	2 3	2" x WOF 2" x WOF (SPU 1)	1 1 1 2	21" (SPU 5) 17" (SPU 3) 18" (SPU 4) 1" x 1¼" (S14)
½ yard color 7 green tonal*	1 3 5	1½" x WOF 1¼" x WOF 1" x WOF	4 4 10 4 10 4 7 10 6 4 4 4	2" (S13) 5" (S11) 3½" (S10) 2¾" (S9) 2" (S8) 1½" (S12) 8" (S7) 6½" (S6) 5" (S5) 4¼" (S4) 3½" (S3) 1" R squares

FABRIC Measurements based on 42" (WOF) usable fabric width. S = spacer SPU = strip-pieced unit	#STRIPS & PIECES	CUT	#PIECES	SUBCUT
⅝ yard color 6 lightest blue tonal*	2 3 2 3	2" x WOF 2" x WOF (SPU 1) 1" x 23" Q 1" x WOF P	1 1 1 1 2	21" (SPU 5) 17" (SPU 3) 15" (SPU 2) 18" (SPU 4) 1" x 1¼" (S16)
½ yard color 2 dark blue tonal*	3 2 3	2" x WOF (SPU 1) 1½" x 30" T 1½" x WOF U		
⅞ yard color 1 darkest blue tonal*	4 3 2 2 3	2" x WOF 2" x WOF (SPU 1) 1" x WOF 1½" x 23" O 1½" x WOF N	2 2 2 2 4 12 9	21" (SPU 5) 17" (SPU 3) 15" (SPU 2) 18" (SPU 4) 1¼" (S17) 3½" (S2) 2" (S1)
Backing		36" x 69"		

SUPPLIES

- Batting 36" x 69"
- All-purpose thread to match fabrics
- Quilting thread
- Basic sewing tools and supplies

Project Specifications

Skill Level: Intermediate
Project Size: 29½" x 63"
Technique: Strip piecing

Completing the Main Strip-Pieced Units

1. Select all strips labeled SPU 1. Join one of each color strip with right sides together along length as shown in Figure 1 to make strip-pieced unit (SPU) 1; press seams in one direction. Repeat to make three SPU 1 strip sets.

2. Subcut the SPU 1 strip sets into units, again referring to Figure 1.

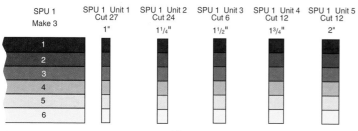

Figure 1

3. Join SPU 2 strips with right sides together along length as shown in Figure 2 to make the SPU 2 strip set; subcut strip set into units, again referring to Figure 2.

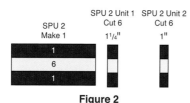

Figure 2

4. Join SPU 3 strips with right sides together along length as shown in Figure 3 to make the SPU 3 strip set; subcut strip set into units, again referring to Figure 3.

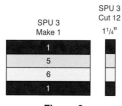

Figure 3

5. Join the SPU 4 strips with right sides together along length as shown in Figure 4 to make the SPU 4 strip set; subcut strip set into units, again referring to Figure 4.

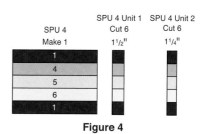

Figure 4

6. Join the SPU 5 strips with right sides together along length as shown in Figure 5 to make the SPU 5 strip set; subcut strip set into units, again referring to Figure 5.

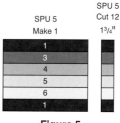

Figure 5

7. Remove piece 6 from an SPU 1 Unit 1 strip and sew to S14 to make K-bottom and K-top units as shown in Figure 6. Repeat to make two of each unit.

8. Remove pieces 5 and 6 from an SPU 1 Unit 1 strip to make L-bottom and L-top units referring to Figure 7. Repeat to make two of each unit.

9. Remove pieces 5 and 6 from an SPU 1 Unit 1 strip and sew to S15 to make M-bottom and M-top units as shown in Figure 8.

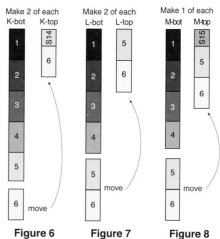

Figure 6   **Figure 7**   **Figure 8**

10. Remove piece 6 from an SPU 1 Unit 2 strip to make J-bottom and J-top units as shown in Figure 9; repeat to make two of each unit.

11. Remove piece 1 from the darkest end of two SPU 1 Unit 5 strips to make two G-top units as shown in Figure 10.

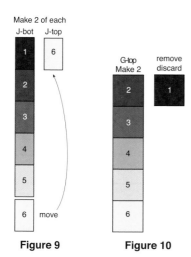

Figure 9 **Figure 10**

and bottom of the pieced center; press seams toward Q-R strips.

6. Join U strips with right sides together on short ends to make one long strip; press seams open. Subcut strip into two 57½" U strips.

7. Sew U strips to opposite long sides and T strips to the top and bottom of the pieced center; press seams toward U and T strips.

Piecing the Rows

Note: Prior to assembling rows, be sure all pieces and units are completed and labeled.

1. Assemble the rows as shown in Figure 11 (page 24), completing two rows each A through L and one M row; press seams in one direction. Mark the top of each row with its designated letter. *Note: Units that require trimming once the quilt center is complete are marked with **.*

2. Assemble the left side of the quilt center, starting with row A through M as shown in Figure 12 (page 25); press seams in one direction.

3. Assemble the right side of the quilt center in reversed order, again referring to Figure 12; press seams in one direction.

4. Join the two pieced sections to complete the quilt center; press seam to one side. Trim I, K and M rows even with the bottom of the pieced center.

Adding Borders

1. Join N strips with right sides together on short ends to make one long strip; press seams open. Subcut strip into two 54½" N strips.

2. Sew N strips to opposite long sides and O strips to the top and bottom of the pieced center; press seams toward N and O strips.

3. Join P strips with right sides together on short ends to make one long strip; press seams open. Subcut strip into two 56½" P strips.

4. Sew P strips to opposite long sides of the pieced center; press seams toward P strips.

5. Sew an R square to each end of each Q strip; press seams toward Q. Sew a Q-R strip to the top

24

Figure 11

Beautiful Bargello

Finishing the Quilt

1. Sandwich batting between the completed top and prepared backing piece; pin or baste layers together to hold flat.

2. Quilt as desired by hand or machine; remove pins or basting. Trim batting and backing even with the top.

3. Join the binding strips with right sides together on short ends to make one long strip; press seams open.

4. Press the strip in half with wrong sides together along length.

5. Sew the binding to the quilt edges, mitering corners and overlapping ends.

6. Fold binding to the back side and stitch in place to finish. ❖

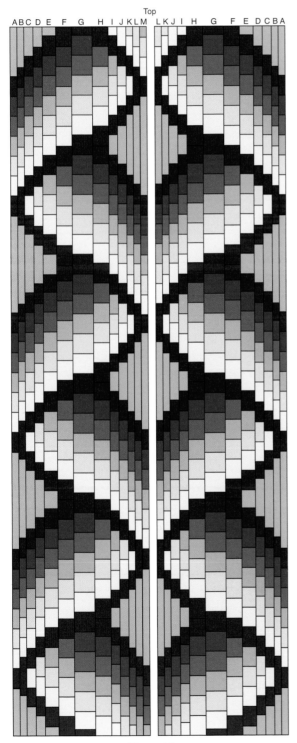

Figure 12

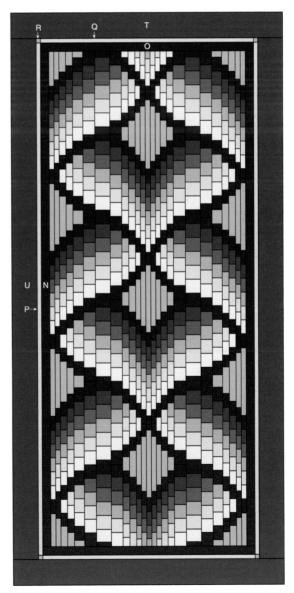

Winter Whisper
Placement Diagram 29¹/₂" x 63"

Candy Hearts

Design by Colleen Reale & Chloe Anderson for Toadusew

Sewn by Lyndell Simmon; Quilted by Asta Dorset

Bargello strips combine to make heart-design blocks in this beautiful quilt.

Designer Notes

Labeling and organizing pieces and units as they are listed will prevent confusion later.

An accurate ¼" seam allowance is critical when strip-piecing and should be verified prior to sewing.

Press seams open to reduce bulk.

Use a smaller stitch length (1.5–2.0) to provide stability.

To avoid confusion, mark the top and bottom units of each row with its designated letter and location; i.e., A TOP and A BOT. This will assist in row positioning and seam directions when assembling the blocks.

Make 18 rows each of the following: A–I. Make nine of row J.

The abbreviations used in instructions are SPU (strip-pieced unit) and S (spacer).

Project Specifications

Skill Level: Intermediate
Project Size: 103" x 101"
Number of Blocks: 9
Block Size: 30" x 30"
Technique: Strip piecing

Candy Heart
30" x 30" Block
Make 9

Materials

- 1¼ yards dark pink tonal color 2
- 1½ yards medium pink tonal color 3
- 1½ yards green tonal color 6
- 1⅔ yards light pink mottled color 4
- 1⅞ yards lightest pink mottled color 5
- 3 yards burgundy tonal
- 2¾ yards darkest pink tonal color 1
- Batting 109" x 107"
- Backing 109" x 107"
- Neutral color all-purpose thread
- Quilting thread
- Basic sewing tools and supplies

Cutting

1. Cut (26) 3½" by fabric width strips color 1; subcut strips into (36) 1¾" S1 and S3 pieces. Reserve 18 strips for SPU 1 and two strips each for SPU 3, 4 and 5.

2. Cut one 2" by fabric width strip color 1; subcut strip into (18) 2¼" S2 pieces.

3. Cut (11) 3½" by fabric width strips color 2; reserve nine strips for SPU 1 and two for SPU 2.

4. Cut (13) 3½" by fabric width strips color 3; reserve nine strips for SPU 1 and two each for SPU 2 and 3.

5. Cut one 2" by fabric width strip color 3; subcut strip into six 1½" S4 pieces.

6. Cut (15) 3½" by fabric width strips color 4; reserve nine strips for SPU 1 and two each for SPU 2, 3 and 4.

7. Cut one 2" by fabric width strip color 4; subcut strip into (18) 2" S5 pieces.

8. Cut (17) 3½" by fabric width strips color 5; reserve nine strips for SPU 1 and two each for SPU 2, 3, 4 and 5 strips.

9. Cut one 2" by fabric width strip color 5; subcut strip into (18) 2" S6 pieces.

10. Cut one 9½" by fabric width strip color 6; subcut strip into (18) 1¾" S7 pieces.

11. Cut two 6½" by fabric width strips color 6; subcut strip into (18) 2" S8 pieces and (18) 1¾" S13 pieces.

12. Cut one 5" by fabric width strips color 6; subcut strip into (18) 2" S11 pieces.

13. Cut three 3½" by fabric width strips color 6; subcut strips into (36) 2" S9 and S10 pieces and (18) 1¾" S14 pieces.

14. Cut one 2" by fabric width strip color 6; subcut strip into (18) 2" S12 pieces.

15. Cut five 1½" by fabric width strips color 6; subcut strips into six 12½" S17 pieces, nine 8" S15 pieces and nine 5" S16 pieces.

16. Cut (11) 6" by fabric width A/B strips burgundy tonal.

17. Cut (11) 2¼" by fabric width binding strips burgundy tonal.

Completing the Main Strip-Pieced Units (SPU)

1. Select labeled SPU 1 strips.

2. Join strips with right sides together along length as shown in Figure 1 to make one strip-pieced unit (SPU) 1; press seams open. Repeat to make nine SPU 1 strip sets.

3. Subcut the SPU 1 strip sets into units, again referring to Figure 1.

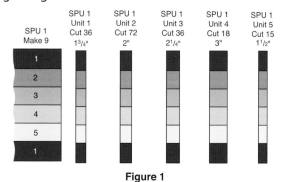

Figure 1

4. Join SPU 2 strips with right sides together along length as shown in Figure 2 to make one SPU 2 strip set; press seams open. Repeat to make two SPU 2 strip sets. Subcut strip sets into units, again referring to Figure 2.

5. Join SPU 3 strips with right sides together along length as shown in Figure 3 to make one SPU 3 strip set; press seams open. Repeat to make two SPU 3

strip sets; subcut strip sets into units, again referring to Figure 3.

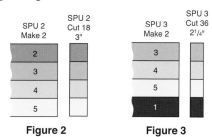

Figure 2   **Figure 3**

6. Join the SPU 4 strips with right sides together along length as shown in Figure 4 to make one SPU 4 strip set; press seams open. Repeat to make two SPU 4 strip sets; subcut strip sets into units, again referring to Figure 4.

Figure 4

7. Join the SPU 5 strips with right sides together along length as shown in Figure 5 to make one SPU 5 strip set; press seams open. Repeat to make two SPU 5 strip sets; subcut strip sets into units, again referring to Figure 5.

Figure 5

8. Cut one SPU 1, Unit 1 as shown in Figure 6 and label A-BOT and A-TOP; repeat to make 18 of each unit.

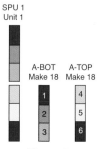

Figure 6

9. Cut one SPU 1, Unit 2 as shown in Figure 7; trim 1½" off piece 4 and label B-BOT. Add S5 to the color 5 end and label B-TOP. Repeat to make 18 of each unit.

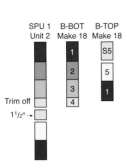

Figure 7

10. Cut one SPU 1, Unit 2 as shown in Figure 8; label C-BOT and C-TOP. Repeat to make 18 of each unit.

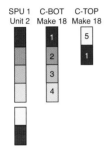

Figure 8

11. Cut one SPU 1, Unit 3 strip as shown in Figure 9; trim 1½" off piece 5 and label D-BOT. Add S6 to the color 1 piece and label D-TOP. Repeat to make 18 of each unit.

12. Cut one SPU 1, Unit 5 as shown in Figure 10; trim 1½" off piece 3 and label Sashing BOT. Add S4 to the color 4 end and label Sashing TOP. Repeat to make six of each unit.

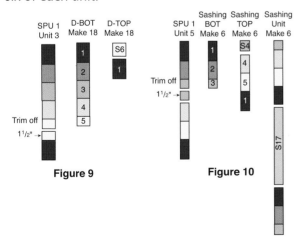

Figure 9

Figure 10

13. Sew sashing TOP to sashing BOT with S17, again referring to Figure 10; repeat to make six sashing units.

14. Trim 1½" off the color 1 end of one SPU 3 and label F-BOT as shown in Figure 11; repeat to make 18 units.

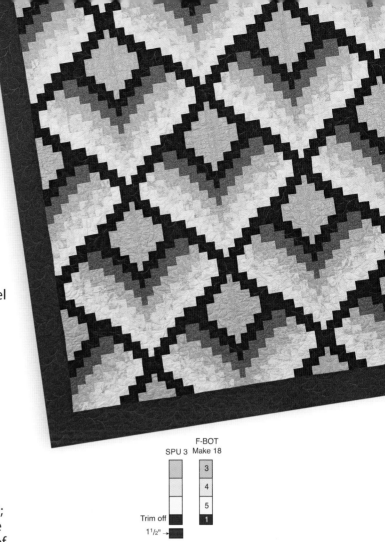

Figure 11

Completing the Candy Heart Blocks

1. Arrange and join the TOP and BOT units with S pieces and SPU units to make rows as shown in Figure 12; press seams open. Repeat to make 18 each A–I rows and nine J rows.

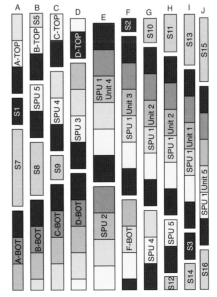

Figure 12

2. Join A–I rows to make a left-side unit and I–A rows to make a right-side unit as shown in Figure 13. Join the units with a J row to complete one Candy Heart block, again referring to Figure 13; press seams open. Repeat to make nine blocks. *Note: Arrows indicate sewing direction for joining the rows.*

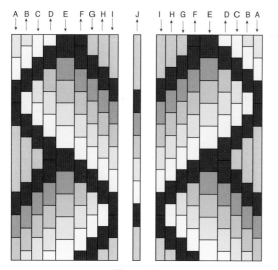

Figure 13

Completing the Top

1. Join three Candy Heart blocks with two sashing units to make a row as shown in Figure 14; press seams open. Repeat to make three rows.

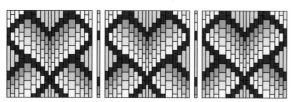

Figure 14

2. Join the rows to complete the pieced center; press seams open.

3. Join the A/B strips on short ends to make one long strip; press seams open. Subcut strip into two 104" A strips and two 106" B strips.

4. Center and sew A strips to opposite sides and B strips to the top and bottom of the pieced center, stopping stitching ¼" from each end.

5. Stitch end seams at a 45-degree angle to make a mitered corner; trim mitered seam to ¼" and press open to complete the pieced top. Press seams toward A and B strips.

Finishing the Quilt

1. Sandwich batting between the completed top and prepared backing piece; pin or baste layers together to hold flat.

2. Quilt as desired by hand or machine; remove pins or basting. Trim batting and backing even with the top.

3. Join the binding strips with right sides together on short ends to make one long strip; press seams open.

4. Press the strip in half with wrong sides together along length.

5. Sew the binding to the quilt edges, mitering corners and overlapping ends.

6. Fold binding to the back side and stitch in place to finish. ❖

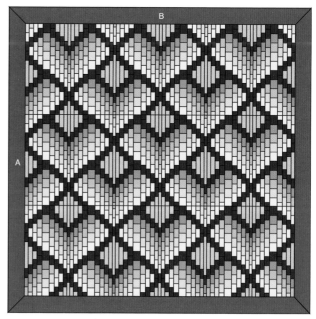

Candy Hearts
Placement Diagram 103" x 101"

Snowflake Jewels

By Ann Lauer

Try the quilt-as-you-go technique when making this elegant bargello runner.

Designer Notes

I find it helpful to cut a swatch of each fabric and staple it to a piece of paper and number appropriately. This helps me keep the fabrics, which are very close in color, in order.

Project Specifications

Skill Level: Beginner
Project Size: 54¼" x 20"
Technique: Tube piecing

Materials

- ⅛ yard white with silver metallic for appliqué
- ¼ yard each 8 blue mottleds from lightest (fabric 2) to darkest (fabric 9)
- ¼ yard white tonal (fabric 1)
- ⅝ yard navy mottled (fabric 10)
- ¾ yard gridded flannel
- Batting 59" x 26"
- Backing 59" x 26"
- Neutral color and white all-purpose thread
- Quilting thread
- ½ yard lightweight fusible web
- Hot-fix crystals
- Iridescent art glitter
- Quilter's safety pins or basting spray
- Basic sewing tools and supplies

Cutting

1. Press and straighten fabrics for cutting.

2. Cut two 2½" by fabric width strips from each of the 10 numbered fabrics.

3. Cut four 2¼" by fabric width strips navy mottled for binding.

Preparing Tubes

1. Arrange 2½" strips in numerical order from lightest (1) to darkest (10).

2. Join one set of strips with right sides together along length in numerical order using a ¼" seam allowance to make a strip set as shown in Figure 1; press seams toward fabric 1. Repeat to make two strip sets, pressing seams of second strip set toward fabric 10. ***Note:*** *When pressing, press first from the wrong side and then from the right side.*

Figure 1

3. Join long edges of one strip set with right sides together along length to make a tube as shown in Figure 2; press seam in same direction as other seams in the tube. Repeat with the second strip set.

Figure 2

Preparing Backing & Batting

1. Place the backing piece wrong side up on a flat surface.

2. Lay the gridded flannel with the grid facing the backing; align the grid line even with the top and left edges of the fabric. ***Note:*** *You may use a combination of flannel and very thin batting.* Lay the batting on top of the flannel. You should be able to see the grid lines through the batting but not so much that they show through the lightest fabric.

3. If not using gridded flannel, draw a straight line from top to bottom 2" in from the left edge; continue drawing lines every 4" across the batting. Draw a horizontal line across the top 2" in from the edge; continue drawing lines every 6" below it.

4. Secure the layers with basting spray or with safety pins every 10", pinning on the flannel/batting side.

Cutting the Strip Tubes

1. Lay the stitched tubes wrong sides out on a cutting mat, carefully folding on a seam line. Label one Odd and the other Even.

2. Referring to Figure 3 for sizes to cut, cut each tube into 18 segments, cutting odd-numbered cuts from the Odd tube and even-numbered cuts from the Even tube to ensure that the opposing seams will nest together as they are sewn; straighten as needed when cutting. Label each segment with the segment number shown in the chart; arrange segments in numerical order.

3. Open each segment at the seam indicated in the chart. For example: For segment 1, open seam 1—the seam between fabric 1 (white) and fabric 2 (lightest blue). For segment 2, open seam 2; for segment 3, open seam 3, etc. Be sure to pay close attention to the chart when opening seams. Seams are not always opened in numerical order.

4. Lay segment 1 on the batting even with the vertical line at top left and with the top of fabric 2 even with the top horizontal line (approximately 2" from the top and left raw edges of the fabric/batting) as shown in Figure 4. Fabric 1 will be at the bottom; pin in place. Stitch ⅛" from left edge to anchor in place.

Figure 4

5. Place segment 2 right sides together with segment 1 with fabric 3 at the top and fabric 2 at the bottom as shown in Figure 5; match strip seams from segment 1 to segment 2 and align on top and right edges, again referring to Figure 5. Pin at each seam.

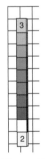

Figure 5

6. Stitch the seam through all layers including batting and backing; carefully

Segment No.	Odd Cut Width	Separate on seam	Segment No.	Even Cut Width	Separate on seam
1	1¼"	1	2	1¾"	2
3	1½"	3	4	2¼"	4
5	2"	5	6	3"	6
7	2½"	7	8	2¾"	8
9	3¾"	9	10	4¼"	10
11	3"	9	12	2¼"	8
13	1½"	7	14	1½"	6
15	1¼"	5	16	1"	4
17	¾"	3	18	¾"	2
19	1"	3	20	2"	4
21	2¼"	5	22	1¾"	6
23	1½"	7	24	1"	8
25	¾"	9	26	1"	8
27	1¼"	7	28	2"	6
29	3	5	30	3½"	4
31	2½"	5	32	2"	6
33	1½"	7	34	1¾"	6
35	3	5	36	3½"	6

Figure 3

fold segment 2 open as shown in Figure 6 and lightly press it flat.

Figure 6

7. Repeat steps 5 and 6 to add all segments.

8. As you lay each new segment on the previous segment, pin carefully and be sure that the top edges align with the top horizontal line. As you open the segments, the cut edge should be parallel to the vertical registration lines. If the segments are beginning to slant or bow, make a slight adjustment (sew a slightly wider or narrower seam) as soon as possible—make the adjustments on the wider strips so that they are less noticeable.

9. As you join the segments, compare your design with Figure 7 and the project photo to be sure that you are shifting the strips correctly.

10. Stitch ⅛" from the right side edge of the final segment.

11. Use a large square template or right-angle ruler to check that your runner is square; straighten as needed. Trim batting, flannel and backing even with the top.

Finishing the Runner

1. Join the binding strips with right sides together on short ends to make one long strip; press seams open.

2. Press the strip in half with wrong sides together along length.

3. Sew the binding to the quilt edges, mitering corners and overlapping ends.

4. Fold binding to the back side and stitch in place to finish.

5. Trace the outline of each snowflake onto the paper side of the fusible web. *Note: We have shared six different snowflake designs; you may use as many of each one as you desire.*

6. Cut out shapes, leaving a margin around each one; fuse shapes to the wrong side of the white with silver metallic. Cut out shapes on traced lines; remove paper backing.

7. Arrange and fuse snowflake shapes on the quilted runner as desired, referring to the Placement Diagram and project photo for positioning suggestions.

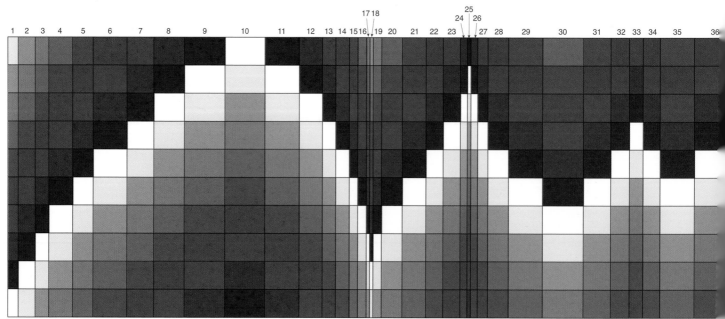

Figure 7

8. Stitch shapes in place close to edges with white thread. Add art glitter and hot-fix crystals as desired referring to manufacturer's instructions. ❖

Snowflake Jewels
Placement Diagram 54¼" x 20"

Snowflake Patterns
Cut as desired from white with silver metallic

House of White Birches, Berne, Indiana 46711   DRGnetwork.com

Rugged High Country

By Ann Lauer

Make a landscape scene by shifting stitched strips
up and down using the quilt-as-you-go method.

Designer Notes

Because there are 17 fabrics used in the bargello portion of this quilt, I find it helpful to cut a swatch of each fabric and staple it to a piece of paper and number appropriately. This helps me keep the fabrics, which are very close in color, in order.

Fabric 1 is the green grass; the next 10 fabrics are a variety of greens that get progressively darker in value. You may add green fabrics that include golds and browns—any colors that are found in a forest. Batiks work well. Fabric 11 is the darkest green; fabrics 12–15 are grays that shade from dark to light. Fabric 16 is white for the snowcap and fabric 17 is the blue sky.

The rocks were cut from one batik fabric and the bears were cut from another. Rock and pebble prints were fussy-cut to create realistic details. These may be arranged as desired after cutting.

It is difficult to make an exact copy of a landscape quilt with lots of little appliqué details. Make this quilt your own by adding or taking away motifs.

Project Specifications

Skill Level: Intermediate
Project Size: 52" x 44"
Technique: Strip piecing

Materials

- Scrap medium green for tree 1
- ⅛ yard medium blue mottled for lake shadow
- ⅛ yard gray/brown mottled for rocks
- ⅛ yard pebble print
- ⅛ yard white/gray mottled for clouds
- ¼ yard brown mottled for bears
- ¼ yard blue mottled for lake
- ¼ yard each green fabric 2–8 and 10 progressing from light to dark
- ¼ yard dark gray/green (fabric 12)
- ¼ yard each light (fabric 15), medium (fabric 14) and dark (fabric 13) gray
- ¼ yard white (fabric 16)
- ⅜ yard green (fabric 9) fitting into the light-to-dark progression between fabrics 8 and 10
- ¾ yard deep green (fabric 11) fitting into the end of the light-to-dark progression after fabric 10
- 1⅛ yards blue-sky print (fabric 17)
- 1¼ yards light green (fabric 1)
- 1½ yards gridded flannel
- Thin batting 58" x 50"
- Backing 58" x 50"
- Neutral color all-purpose thread
- All-purpose thread to match appliqués
- Quilting thread
- ½ yard lightweight fusible web
- Quilter's safety pins or basting spray
- Basic sewing tools and supplies

Cutting

1. Press and straighten fabrics for cutting.

2. Cut two 20" by fabric width strips fabric 1 and two 16" by fabric width strips fabric 17.

3. Cut two 2" by fabric width strips from the other 15 numbered fabrics.

4. Cut five 2¼" by fabric width strips from the remainder of fabric 11 for binding.

5. Trace appliqué pieces onto the paper side of the fusible web using patterns given; cut as directed on each piece. Cut out shapes, leaving a margin around each one.

6. Fuse shapes to the wrong side of fabrics as directed on patterns for color; cut out shapes on traced lines. Remove paper backing.

7. Cut clusters of pebbles from the pebble print as desired.

Preparing Strips

1. Arrange 2", 16" and 20" strips in numerical order from lightest (1) to darkest (17).

2. Join one set of strips with right sides together along length in numerical order using a ¼" seam allowance

Odd			Even		
Segment No.	Cut Width	Shift	Segment No.	Cut Width	Shift
1	4½"		2	3½"	up
3	2½"	up	4	1½"	up
5	1¼"	up	6	1"	up
7	1"	up	8	1"	up
9	1½"	down	10	1½"	down
11	1¾"	down	12	1¾"	down
13	1¾"	down	14	1½"	down
15	1¼"	down	16	1¼"	down
17	3¼"	down	18	1¾"	up
19	1½"	up	20	1½"	up
21	2¼"	down	22	2½"	down
23	3"	up	24	3½"	up
25	4"	up	26	5¼"	up
27	3¼"	down	28	2¼"	down
29	2¼	down	30	2¼"	down

Figure 2

to make a strip set as shown in Figure 1 and referring to the "Joining Strips" sidebar; press seams toward fabric 1. Repeat to make two strip sets, pressing seams of second strip set toward fabric 17. *Note: When pressing, press first from the wrong side and then from the right side.*

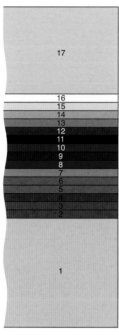

Figure 1

Preparing Backing & Batting

1. Place the backing piece wrong side up on a flat surface.

2. Center the gridded flannel with the grid facing the backing; align the grid line even with the top and left edges of the fabric. Lay the batting on top of the flannel. You should be able to see the grid lines through the batting, but not so much that they show through the lightest fabric.

3. If you are not using gridded flannel, draw a straight line from top to bottom 2" in from the left edge; continue drawing lines every 4" across the batting. Draw a horizontal line across the top 2" down from the edge; continue drawing lines every 6" below it.

4. Secure the layers with basting spray or with safety pins every 10", pinning on the flannel/batting side.

Cutting the Strip Sets

1. Place the stitched strip sets on a cutting mat. Label one Odd and the other Even.

2. Referring to Figure 2 for sizes to cut, cut each strip set into 15 segments, cutting odd-numbered cuts from the Odd strip set and even-numbered cuts from the Even strip set to ensure that the opposing seams will nest together as they are sewn; straighten as needed when cutting. Label each

Joining Strips

To join strips to make strip sets, begin by joining in sets of two. Lay strip 2 on top of strip 1 and then strip 4 on top of strip 3, etc., always laying the even-numbered strip on top of the odd-numbered strip.

Continue until all strips except one have been sewn together in pairs.

Sew all the sets of two together; for example, sew set 3/4 to set 1/2, then set 5/6 onto the combined large section. It is important to always sew with the lower-numbered strips on top and the higher-numbered strips on the bottom. This means that when you are adding set 3/4 to set 1/2, place set 3/4 right sides together on set 1/2. Then flip the sets over and sew together. This joins the strips by stitching in the opposite direction from that used to join the individual strips and will prevent bowing.

As you sew, keep strips even on one end.

Do not pull the strips as you sew them; let them feed through the machine.

segment with the segment number shown in the chart; arrange segments in numerical order.

Assembling & Trimming the Quilt

1. Lay segment 1 on the batting on a grid line 2" in from the left vertical line and with the top of fabric 17 placed 3" above the top horizontal line as shown in Figure 3; pin to hold. Stitch ⅛" from left edge to anchor in place.

2. Place segment 2 right sides together with segment 1, shifting up one position as shown in Figure 4. *Note: The top edge should be approximately 1½" above the top of segment 1. Seam allowances should always be opposing and therefore fit together snugly. From this point on you will shift each segment either up or down one position as directed in Figure 2 charts to give the design movement. The segments should never shift up or down more than one position at a time. As you shift the segments, the top and bottom edges will not be even. These will be squared off at the end.* Pin at each seam.

3. Stitch the seam through all layers including batting and backing; carefully fold segment 2 open as shown in Figure 5 and lightly press it flat.

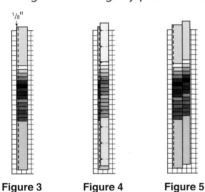

Figure 3   Figure 4   Figure 5

4. Repeat steps 2 and 3 to add all segments.

5. As you lay each new segment on the previous segment, pin carefully to be sure that the seam allowances fit together. As you open the segments, the cut edge should be parallel to the vertical registration lines. If the segments are beginning to slant or bow, make a slight adjustment (sew a slightly wider or narrower seam) as soon as possible—make the adjustments on the wider strips so that they are less noticeable.

6. As you join the segments, compare your design with Figure 6 (page 40) and the project photo to be sure that you are shifting the strips correctly.

7. Stitch ⅛" from the right side edge of the final segment.

8. Using a long right-angle ruler, draw—do not cut—a line across the top and bottom of the quilt

perpendicular to the sides, aligning the ruler with the shortest blue sky strips and shortest green grass strips as shown in Figure 7. Draw vertical lines to straighten the sides, if necessary. Check to be sure your quilt is square; cut on the drawn lines to remove excess.

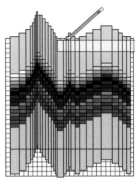

Figure 7

Completing the Appliqué

1. Arrange appliqué shapes on the pieced background referring to the Placement Diagram and project photo for positioning.

2. Using thread to match or contrast with appliqué shapes, straight-stitch around edges to hold in place. Detail lines may be added as desired.

Finishing the Quilt

1. Join the binding strips with right sides together on short ends to make one long strip; press seams open.

2. Press the strip in half with wrong sides together along length.

3. Sew the binding to the quilt edges, mitering corners and overlapping ends.

4. Fold binding to the back side and stitch in place to finish. ❖

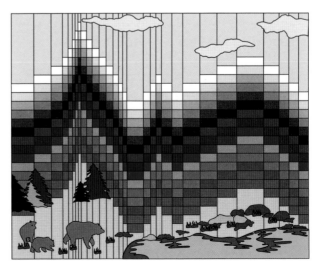

Rugged High Country
Placement Diagram 52" x 44"

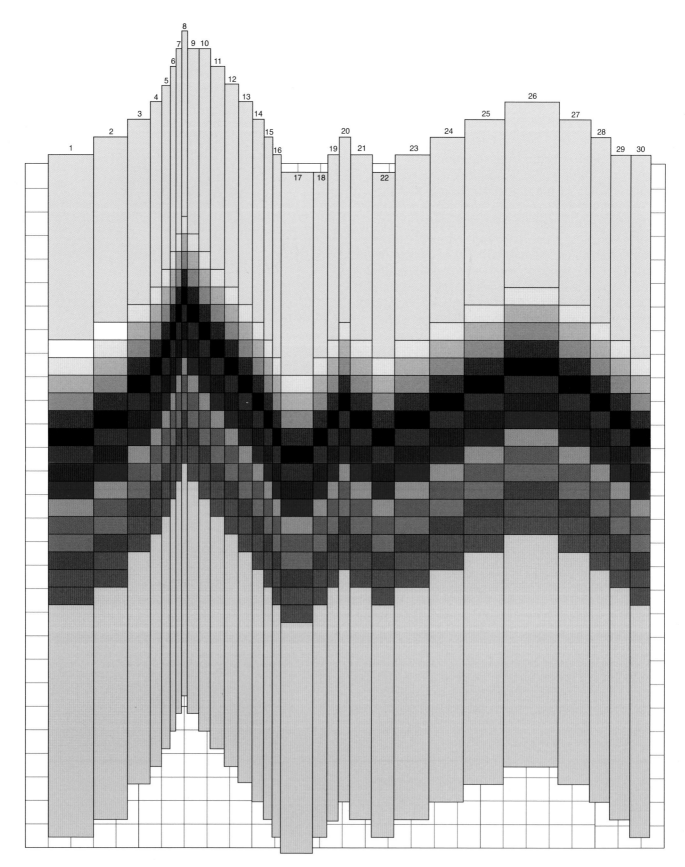

Figure 6

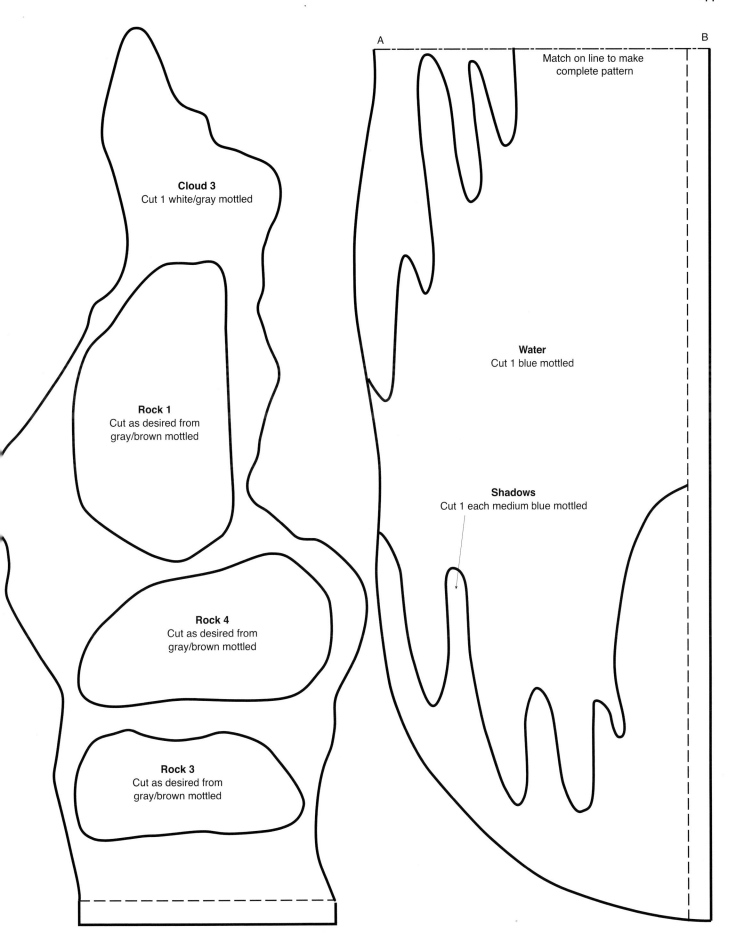

Cloud 3
Cut 1 white/gray mottled

Rock 1
Cut as desired from
gray/brown mottled

Rock 4
Cut as desired from
gray/brown mottled

Rock 3
Cut as desired from
gray/brown mottled

A   B

Match on line to make
complete pattern

Water
Cut 1 blue mottled

Shadows
Cut 1 each medium blue mottled

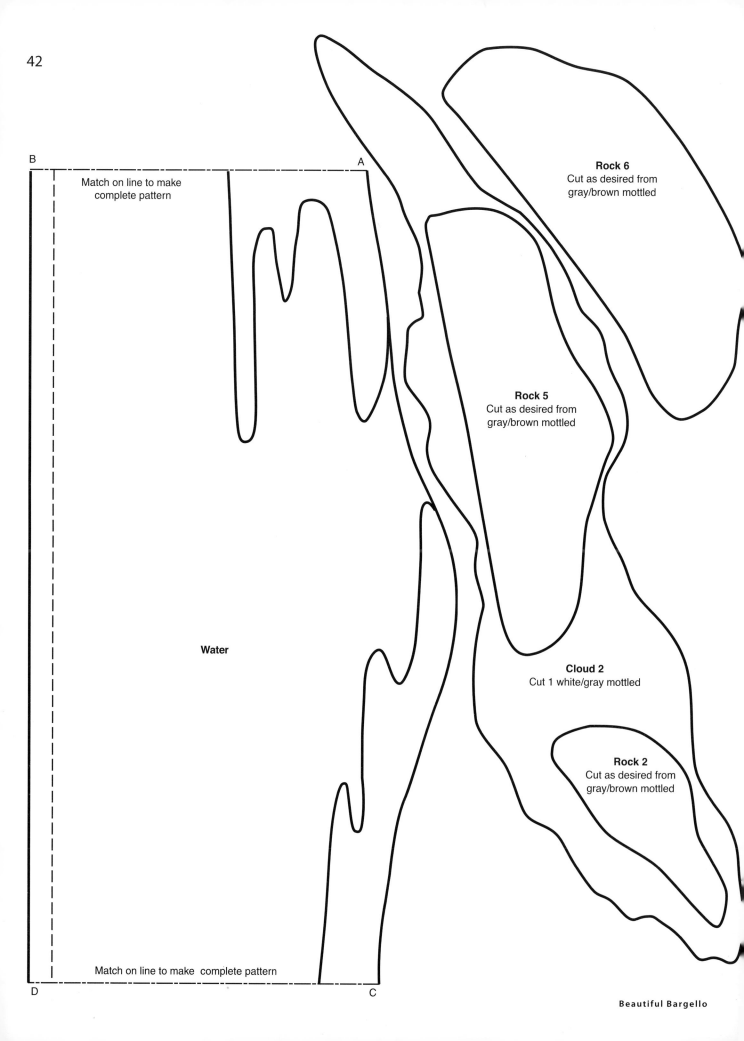

42

B   A

Match on line to make
complete pattern

Rock 6
Cut as desired from
gray/brown mottled

Rock 5
Cut as desired from
gray/brown mottled

Water

Cloud 2
Cut 1 white/gray mottled

Rock 2
Cut as desired from
gray/brown mottled

Match on line to make complete pattern

D   C

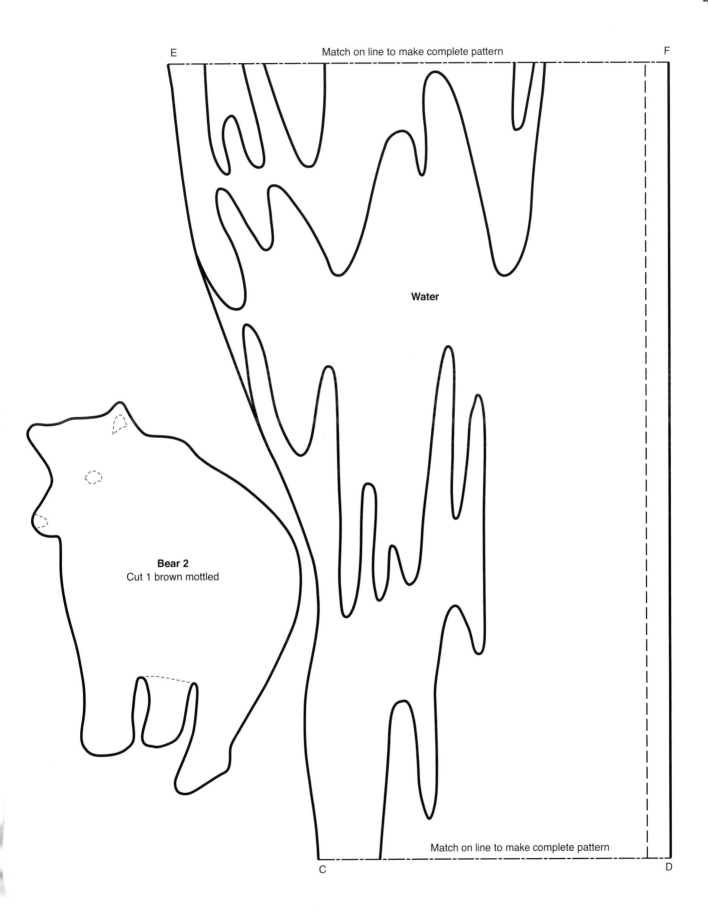

E   Match on line to make complete pattern   F

Water

Bear 2
Cut 1 brown mottled

Match on line to make complete pattern

C   D

House of White Birches, Berne, Indiana 46711   DRGnetwork.com

44

Bear 1
Cut 1 brown mottled

E

Match on line to make complete pattern

Water

F

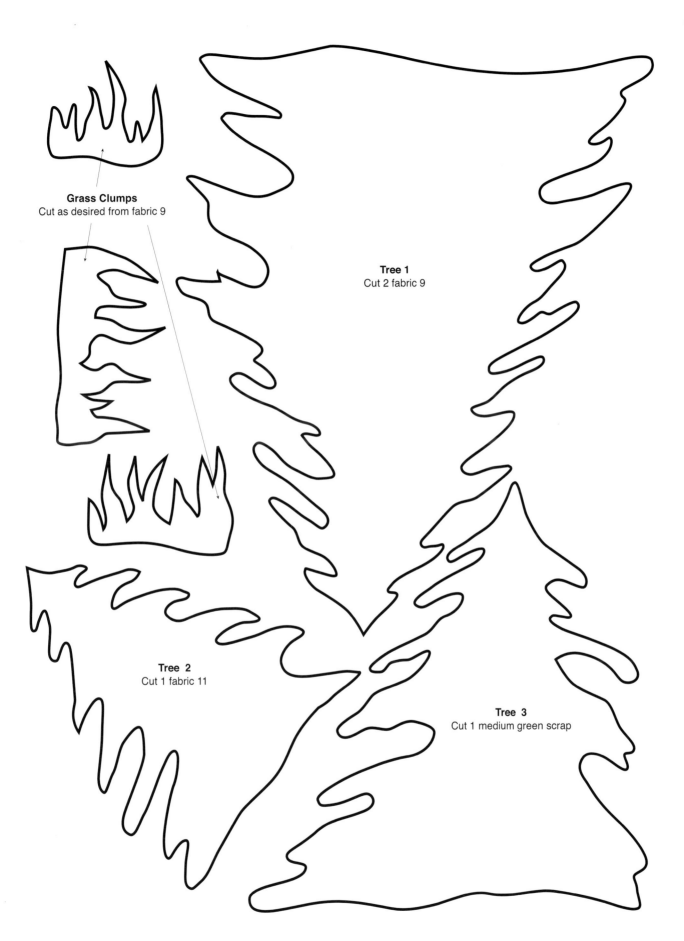

Grass Clumps
Cut as desired from fabric 9

Tree 1
Cut 2 fabric 9

Tree 2
Cut 1 fabric 11

Tree 3
Cut 1 medium green scrap

House of White Birches, Berne, Indiana 46711   DRGnetwork.com

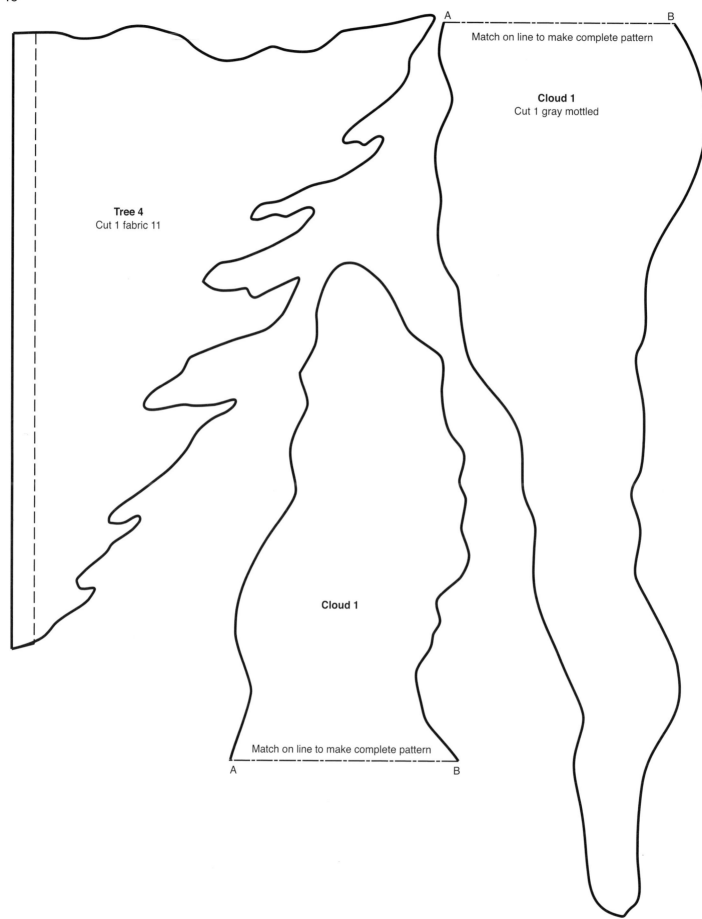

A B

Match on line to make complete pattern

Cloud 1
Cut 1 gray mottled

Tree 4
Cut 1 fabric 11

Cloud 1

Match on line to make complete pattern

A B

Beautiful Bargello

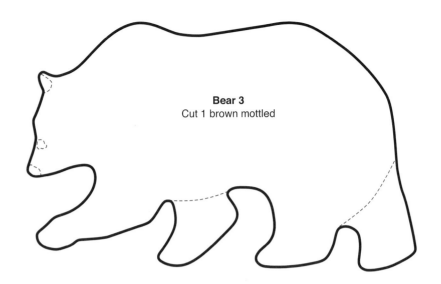

Bear 3
Cut 1 brown mottled

Metric Conversions

Canada/U.S. Measurement				Multiplied by	Metric Measurement
yards	x	.9144	=		metres (m)
yards	x	91.44	=		centimetres (cm)
inches	x	2.54	=		centimetres (cm)
inches	x	25.40	=		millimetres (mm)
inches	x	.0254	=		metres (m)

Canada/U.S. Measurement				Multiplied by	Metric Measurement
centimetres	x	.3937	=		inches
metres	x	1.0936	=		yards

Standard Equivalents

Canada/U.S. Measurement		Metric Measurement		
⅛ inch	=	3.20 mm	=	0.32 cm
¼ inch	=	6.35 mm	=	0.635 cm
⅜ inch	=	9.50 mm	=	0.95 cm
½ inch	=	12.70 mm	=	1.27 cm
⅝ inch	=	15.90 mm	=	1.59 cm
¾ inch	=	19.10 mm	=	1.91 cm
⅞ inch	=	22.20 mm	=	2.22 cm
1 inches	=	25.40 mm	=	2.54 cm
⅛ yard	=	11.43 cm	=	0.11 m
¼ yard	=	22.86 cm	=	0.23 m
⅜ yard	=	34.29 cm	=	0.34 m
½ yard	=	45.72 cm	=	0.46 m
⅝ yard	=	57.15 cm	=	0.57 m
¾ yard	=	68.58 cm	=	0.69 m
⅞ yard	=	80.00 cm	=	0.80 m
1 yard	=	91.44 cm	=	0.91 m
1⅛ yard	=	102.87 cm	=	1.03 m
1¼ yard	=	114.30 cm	=	1.14 m

Canada/U.S. Measurement				Metric Measurement		
1⅜ yard	=	125.73 cm	=	1.26 m
1½ yard	=	137.16 cm	=	1.37 m
1⅝ yard	=	148.59 cm	=	1.49 m
1¾ yard	=	160.02 cm	=	1.60 m
1⅞ yard	=	171.44 cm	=	1.71 m
2 yards	=	182.88 cm	=	1.83 m
2⅛ yards	=	194.31 cm	=	1.94 m
2¼ yards	=	205.74 cm	=	2.06 m
2⅜ yards	=	217.17 cm	=	2.17 m
2½ yards	=	228.60 cm	=	2.29 m
2⅝ yards	=	240.03 cm	=	2.40 m
2¾ yards	=	251.46 cm	=	2.51 m
2⅞ yards	=	262.88 cm	=	2.63 m
3 yards	=	274.32 cm	=	2.74 m
3⅛ yards	=	285.75 cm	=	2.86 m
3¼ yards	=	297.18 cm	=	2.97 m
3⅜ yards	=	308.61 cm	=	3.09 m
3½ yards	=	320.04 cm	=	3.20 m
3⅝ yards	=	331.47 cm	=	3.31 m
3¾ yards	=	342.90 cm	=	3.43 m
3⅞ yards	=	354.32 cm	=	3.54 m
4 yards	=	365.76 cm	=	3.66 m
4⅛ yards	=	377.19 cm	=	3.77 m
4¼ yards	=	388.62 cm	=	3.89 m
4⅜ yards	=	400.05 cm	=	4.00 m
4½ yards	=	411.48 cm	=	4.11 m
4⅝ yards	=	422.91 cm	=	4.23 m
4¾ yards	=	434.34 cm	=	4.34 m
4⅞ yards	=	445.76 cm	=	4.46 m
5 yards	=	457.20 cm	=	4.57 m

House of White Birches, Berne, Indiana 46711   DRGnetwork.com

Photo Index

Fabric & Supplies

Pages 6 and 12: Mirage and Diamond Lites—
Shadow Play and Solitaire Whites fabric collections
from Maywood Studio.

Page 21: Winter Whisper—
Fusions fabrics from Robert Kauffman.

Page 26: Candy Hearts—
Jinny Beyer Palette fabric collection from RJR Fabrics.

Pages 31 &36: Snowflake Jewels and Rugged High
Country—Thermore batting from Hobbs and
Creative Grid flannel from Maywood Studio.

E-mail: Customer_Service@whitebirches.com

HOUSE of WHITE BIRCHES
PUBLISHERS
SINCE 1947

Beautiful Bargello is published by DRG, 306 East Parr Road,
Berne, IN 46711, telephone (260) 589-4000. Printed in USA.
Copyright © 2009 DRG. All rights reserved. This publication may
not be reproduced in part or in whole without written permis-
sion from the publisher.

RETAIL STORES: If you would like to carry this pattern book
or any other DRG publications, call the Wholesale Department
at Annie's Attic to set up a direct account: (903) 636-4303. Also,
request a complete listing of publications available from DRG.

Every effort has been made to ensure that the instructions
in this pattern book are complete and accurate. We cannot,
however, take responsibility for human error, typographical
mistakes or variations in individual work.

STAFF

Editors: Jeanne Stauffer, Sandra L. Hatch
Managing Editor: Dianne Schmidt
Technical Artist: Connie Rand
Copy Supervisor: Michelle Beck
Copy Editors: Amanda Ladig,
Mary O'Donnell
Graphic Arts Supervisor:
Ronda Bechinski
Graphic Artists: Pam Gregory,
Erin Augsburger
Art Director: Brad Snow
Assistant Art Director: Nick Pierce
Photography Supervisor:
Tammy Christian
Photography: Scott Campbell
Photo Stylist: Martha Coquat

ISBN: 978-1-59217-252-8

456789